LETTING GRAVITY SPEAK

POEMS

by

Erika Michael

Finishing Line Press
Georgetown, Kentucky

LETTING GRAVITY SPEAK

POEMS

Copyright © 2023 by Erika Michael
ISBN 979-8-88838-182-3 First Edition
All rights reserved under International and Pan-American Copyright Conventions. No part of this book may be reproduced in any manner whatsoever without written permission from the publisher, except in the case of brief quotations embodied in critical articles and reviews.

Publisher: Leah Huete de Maines
Editor: Christen Kincaid
Cover Photos: Erika Michael
Author Photo: Isabelle Quinn
Cover Design: Elizabeth Maines McCleavy

Order online: www.finishinglinepress.com
also available on amazon.com

Author inquiries and mail orders:
Finishing Line Press
P. O. Box 1626
Georgetown, Kentucky 40324
U. S. A.

Table of Contents

WE WALKED 1

like the speed of our years

WE RAILROAD JUNKIES 5
MOUNT SHASTA IN THE MOONLIGHT 7
ES WAR DAS SCHÖNSTE AUF DER WELT 8
SITTING KITTY-CORNER 9
FLOATING WORLD 10
SUNDOWN 11
YOM KIPPUR: OCTOBER 8, 2011 12
DO NOT GO GENTLY 13
DIGITAL ART 14
"OYOYOY TAKE ME HOME WITH YOU" 16
SINCE YOU MOVED TO SKILLED NURSING 17
MY BIRD 18
ARE WE THERE YET 19
ERIKA DON'T LET ME DIE 21
LETTING GRAVITY SPEAK 22

your body, that splendid machine

SOME CRUMBS 25
UNIFIED FIELD 27
VITRUVIAN MAN 28
I DIG MY FEET IN THE SAND 29
YOUR DEATH MASK 30
THAT'S MY DADDY 31
SILENCE 32
I SWORE IT WAS YOU 33
EVEN TODAY 34
SO I'M OFF TO MAUI 35

DID YOU KNOW THAT WE EMBRACED	36
WIDOWS' MANTRA	37
BEHOLD, YOU ARE CONSECRATED TO ME	38
RELICS AND CRYPTIC THINGS	39
BORN HOLDING HANDS	40
YOU LOVED THE TWO AMADEOS	41
ONE CORNER MA!	43
SOME LET GO OF BONES	45
ENTANGLEMENT	46
SWINGIN' ON A STAR	48
MOON BEANS IN A JAR	49
I WANT	50

some notes in infinite dimension

THE PURPOSE OF THIS NOTE
THE FERRY UNYOKES FROM THE PIER AGAIN	53
WE HOVER ON A CLOUD-SLURRIED SOUND	54
HALF-A-CENTURY OF SPRING'S RECOMPENSE	55
CROWS—MY TRUSTY FOOTFRIENDS RISE	56
RATTLESNAKE MOUNTAIN, DUBBED FOR	57
THE AFTER-THAW… CHEESE FONDU	58
I CROSS THE GANG-PLANK'S OLD STEEL	59
THE SUN'S GLIMMER ON THE SOUND	60

ACKNOWLEDGMENTS	61
APPRECIATION	62
ABOUT THE AUTHOR	63

In memory of
Ernest A. Michael

WE WALKED

I couldn't toss your tennis shoes, taupe and tattered,
holes around the toes. They sit in the garage on
cartons of your reprints, going nowhere. You howled
don't let me die rolling down halls of memory care
looking for any exit but *that* one, craving the old beat
of here to there, time-etched footfalls, jive of our

lives tapped out on concrete as we'd head off to
your old co-op on Central Park West throwing the
best in us on to those NY pavements, gratifying
our craving for the Mandelbrot flavors of that city's
fare, amble to the Met on 5th, asylum of queens,
kings, idols & saints; the Modern shrine on 53rd,

depot of geometries & whirling pageantries and to
that other Met where heady arias and strings stirred
cadences of our meandering; we hailed the stalwart
Solomonic lion sentries seated at the entry to our
legendary Library where we'd basked under lamps
that lit the synapses of generations. We refugees

traced our ancestral footfalls to the daisy-dappled
knolls of Lucerne cows, old footbridges and viaducts;
we rode Swiss trains to hobble over cobbles, haunted
Basel hostels for a warm *raclette* with pickles n'
a boiled potato and stalls hawking *Gianduja* the truffle,
sweeter than *Sachertorte* conceived in Vienna,

as I had been—city of that ever-descending wheel
of Harry Lime renown by the coffee-dappled
Danube lulled in the *Schlag* of history. We slogged
the tulip fields of Kuekenhof, saw godly scintillation
in Van Eyck's *Mystic Lamb* and stroked Rabbi Loew's
lions by the mud of the Vlatava. Glad to be home

in the Northwest we hiked cedar-scented switchbacks
through cascades of glacier lily—*trillium* and *saxifrage*

on local trails by the Skycomish, wandered sweeps
of Skagit Valley crocus and narcissus, cherry drifts of
two Washingtons blushing with *yoshino,* and scaled
our Woodway hills whose streets honor First Nations—

the Chinook, Wachusett, Bella Coola and Makah,
we strolled the hills of Pine looking out on Brackett's
Landing where we scrambled over sand and time
scrubbed logs to see hulls recede in amethyst or
ride a ferry to a grandkids picnic on the Kingston bank.
And then you fell. You fell on gold-flecked granite

as your feet no longer found their footing so we rolled
a walker past rose hips near the salt marsh and inhaled
the gulls. When you smelled neither salt nor gulls
we trundled home. With sundown you conjured walking
as I wheeled you through memory care. *Where are you,
I love you* echoed in those well-mopped halls.

It was a pureed bite, a crumb gone mystifyingly awry,
a howl of loss, a hanging on, the doggedness of our
bond and dread within the curtained ether of an ER
tended by the best of docs, among them Josh, my dumb
grasp as they handed me your watch and moved you to
a unit in the back—your shoes inside a plastic sack.

like the speed of our years

WE RAILROAD JUNKIES

chunneled off on new track
wined, dined, bagpiped, and grooved
    away on Eurostar's inaugural from Waterloo
to a red-carpet brass band greeting
by the mayor of Brussels
  and a fine buffet

of Belgian *gaufrettes*!
Rail buffs know—
    the old world-wide web feeds a hunger,
journeys of polyglot gluttony linking
stalls in halls that hawk the local chow like
  Bahnhoff München's *Currywurst,*

Zürich's cheesy *Heischuechli* and the much-loved
soft *gelato* at Milano Centrale
    smoothing those grand delays in that vaulted hall
where lines spin north to Berlin's
crystaline construction—as byzantine as the old beer
  flowing from Hopfingerbräu's keg with

salt-speckled pretzels.
No rails over the Atlantic yet,
    so we contrail home for the specials at
Penn Station where fast grub satisfies a
grumbling gut until we get rollin'
  on some of those best of trains, rockin' west on

the Lake Shore Limited to catch the smooth
Empire Builder plying roadbeds through
    the continental divide from Windy City
to Emerald City
crossing plains and Rocky Mountain highs as we share
  prime rib and berry pie with other track

junkies in this amethyst terrain, especially that well-loved
breakfast as the morning sky

      shines on gold-yolked eggs and grits fixed
like they'd been ladled from some folks' farm kitchen
we'd just whizzed by,
    like the speed of our years.

MOUNT SHASTA IN THE MOONLIGHT

It was the
ta ke ta ke te ka
  ping

that clattered us along miles of track
on Mount Shasta's needle-bed
of old growth—

look up, I said
smile

to capture
a drift of silver sage visible
over a crumple
of *New York Times,*
eyes melted to contentment
in the wood cage of
a superliner whose bed-pillows
couched the coupled bond of a strong
undercarriage—

the squeal of sheen,
the braking and acceleration,
the rushing past streams and banks
slanted to stone, rust
and timber,
generations glimpsed from
fast-forward window-bays synced
to wires strung like
staves of musical code across
a scrim of aspen fading
to dark.

As the moon danced arcs
we rolled in the light cast off Shasta's
pinnacles,
rocking to the track of
ta ke ta ke te ka
  ping

ES WAR DAS SCHÖNSTE AUF DER WELT,

that train ride across the Pyrenees which
brought us to Bilbao, known 'til recent years for
Bill's old *Balhaus* where a dollar rocked a score,
the moon glinted red through the roof n'
grass sprouted from the floor.

But we hadn't come chasing Brechtian dreams—
we came to groove to Ghery's rolling swells
when the sun fell on titanium vaults welling violet
as evening surges sent moonlight over the skin
of that miraculous pile risen on the Nervión.

Inside the swirling core we boogied to the *aha*
rambling among and around 'the usual suspects'
some fine *ancien chapeau* in their venerable way,
Rothko, Serra, Holzer, we'd met them before—
but that day ambling outside under the spell

of this shift-of-the-architype shrine erected
to the glory of art, we saw that it was *swell*—
the most beautiful building in the world, we felt
es war das schönste, es war das schönste,
es war das schönste, auf der Welt

SITTING KITTY-CORNER

from the Carlyle in Cafe Boulud,
I think on afternoons at Bemelman's
with witty Ferdinand of blessed
memory. How we loved to meet

your Frankfurt buddy for high tea—
what pleasure to enjoy his repartee.
Sweet gentleman, he'd spark a ton
of anecdotal memory. I recollect

the day that conversation strayed
like vines on stony walls with empty
spots. We talked some politics,
some family lore. His wife filled in

the gaps of what was said and what
was not—untangled after from before.
He uttered little that last day, smiled
gently, so we took him at his word.

Between the lines there was a metaphor.
That's all there is. There isn't any more.

FLOATING WORLD

Seaside waders cruise among the old
pilings at Brackett's Landing,
blackish blue against a glitter-play of mud flats

this slice of Edmonds's floating world worthy
of Hokusai or Hiroshige—
endless impressions
issued on paper in orange and indigo.

No Mt Fuji here but
to the west, the ragged Olympics—
looking north, Mt Baker—
south, Rainier
climbed years ago by our four sons
rappelling off a single rope,
tiny creatures scaling crags as huge as
the heart of the venture.

We linger here at sunset,
wait for the ferry to reach the pier, its legs creaky
like ours—
the café musters diners for salmon, a local brew,
some loganberry pie
as gulls squawk and scat over green
umbrellas,

scenes framed by the old timbre of this place.

SUNDOWN

fire in the sky
you call,
throwing your arms wide
open toward the glow of twilight
on the Olympics.

We sit by glimmering artifacts
gathered one by one from generations
of Jewish lives.

The trip we booked following the
sun years ago bound for Union Station
ended here on the bluff above the tracks
by the Sound on Chinook—
in our veins the familiar
clack clack squeal of rolling stock
hauled on old rails spun out by field,
river, woodland, poppies,
bridges rising in mist—a life's span—
and ties on the roadbed
secured with spikes and weathered
with love of the journey.

I used to live here
you declare,
seeing flame reflected in the breakfront
where silver candleholders shimmer,
chased and hammered
with gilt.

YOM KIPPUR: OCTOBER 8, 2011

Most folks out and about
this afternoon are untroubled by
calls to repentance as they gaze off decks
over the Sound on Pine.

We pause at a lookout on the hill
where you shiver in the chill of the late
autumn sun. I wrap you in a shawl,
tuck it in your wheelchair.

Avinu malkeinu's crystalline light
washes the wetland sanctuary below and
the white marina where pleasure boats rock
awaiting flight to the San Juans.

Last year we sat in synagogue,
eyes shut for the sorrowful resonance
of *Kol Nidre* imprinted in our marrow's
coil. This year herons cray

as we stand in awe below clouds
out of which God's rays spill over salt
marsh pools mirroring their pewter
undersides. Swamped with prayer,

atonement rises from the grass bent by
summer's excess, wetland drone, and from
the thorns of orange rose-hip fatter than plums
that signify fall reckoning.

Jonah's gourd's withered in a pot by
the gate—we linger underneath the clamor
of gulls, see ferries rumble foam into
the dock, and inhale its kelp.

DO NOT GO GENTLY

With Bro you lay beneath the Chinese scholars'
table, old golden retriever, he chasing marmots
in a dream, and you, hounding proofs with legs.
You puppies riffed your reveries in infinite

dimension, time-warp memories over brilliant
fields and curious spaces. With cerebellar
eloquence you skipped around the billiard
table caroming balls off the grid of your mind's

vectors, champion of cushion-kissing, master
of body English. How you bopped your backspin
tangos at the table tennis tourney—titleholder,
your span of reach and stance could not

portend that final hydrocephalic dance. You
were the genius kid who beat Grandmaster Euwe
in a simul play—was it King's Gambit left you
open to amazing options, vision's where it's at—

took their synchro-breath away. You wheeled
to the sun steeped in heat and light 'til plunging
to that unplumbed depth where cerulean freezes
in winter. The day we studied Breughel's *Icarus*

and feasted on *moule frites* at Chez Léon
I sold my soul for rank *civet de lièvre*—oh no!
You ordered *chicorée-frisée.* And in the end,
while Bro ran out to chase his final mole, no way

you'd mosey gently down that rabbit hole.

DIGITAL ART

Our son laid his hand on a sheet
of paper and with the other
rubbed his thumb on a stiff brush spattering
paint around his fingers.

When he raised them,
a nimbus remained: his palm crowned with
five digit-rays,
our progeny's coat of arms.

Forty thousand years ago
a mystic blew red pigment through a quill
over fingers flattened on the walls of
a cave at El Castillo

leaving stencils of hands
that fondled the clay teats of Venus,
stroked holes on bone flutes
and traced bison on calcite crust.

Yesterday a physicist revealed
the boson shimmering in a field of super-rubble.
Mathematician—lost in infinite dimension as
you languish in a wheelchair

pondering the space between my last visit
and the elevator door, wondrously
weep on hearing
that scholars have found the Higgs particle.

Beneath the tympanum of Ste Foy, Conques,
where God's fingers reach out
of clouds into
this illusionary world

a pilgrim enters the sanctuary
to chronicle the whorls of wormholes

which draw souls.
I recall your mantra—*all I need is paper and pencil.*

As any artist can tell you,
it's the departure that reveals the hand.

"OYOYOY TAKE ME HOME WITH YOU"

rings in my gut,
your eyes begging from this improbable
madhouse where you sit, confabulating and
disphagic.

I inhale your breath
broken with glottal catch, bask in the draw of
your fingers on my hair,
tracks my grandfather traced

blessing my head on a platform
at Vienna's South Station, October '39—
goodness held me there.
My nose and mouth's buried in your neck,

day-old stubble grazing my face with intimacy,
a shirtcollar truth to which I cling
steeped in love's bloodbath—
our marriage knot laced

with neurotangles.
Consider the hypothesis *lemme outta here!*
where here is *where?*
and home—never this wretched chair

SINCE YOU MOVED TO SKILLED NURSING

I'm alone with the relics of a forty-six-year marriage
and unhinged illusions of our enduring
togetherness

Evenings the trash bin thunders before me.
Mornings I brew coffee using your rule for optimal
parts of water to grounds,
pay bills, read the paper—no need to
mark essential items.

I crave your puttering,
your white-haired fragrance, creased face near mine,
brown eyes gleaming at the glow of
light on the Olympics,
and if we're lucky—dancing duos of eagles,
and crows.

I climb the stairs to inhale your crisply
laundered shirts.

MY BIRD

> on seeing Annette Messager's dead sparrows in
> *Le Repos Des Pensionnaires*

Wrapped in knitted woolies and
placed by mysterious design on their
sides and backs in orderly rows,
these spindly sparrows doze

scarcely visible beneath their fluff.
No craving for a rag or twig or some
little lark on the fly—they've had
their tid-bits and are free to wing

their stuff in a deeper sky. This one's
special, heartbeat in a brittle chest,
hold him gingerly, don't crush his frame,
give him custard, push his wheelchair,

call his name.

ARE WE THERE YET

Louis Armstrong
chasing memories of something—
   one of those things
a winter wonderland in blue and silver
crackles melting cycles in a
TV cabaret

   hello!
you shout
   hello!
      where are you?

orange scarf, black corduroy,
transparently
I see you flash on
my periphery
and on the fractal screens of our
entwined brains' multiplex.

You scraped the kitchen counter with
your wheelchair
like you grazed the metrobus as

you steered between the
lines and lanes of your mind's peregrinations—
joyful journeys once taken
to boundaries of
infinite dimension,
circuits through nebulae of
decline

a trip to the moon
in cortical canyons riven by wind.

   Bereshith
you chanted

In the beginning
the earth was waste and void
and God decreed that
light

flush the chilling deep
where exquisite roots weave
neurons spiraling strains
of singular seed—

   hello!
you shout
   are we there yet?

ERIKA DON'T LET ME DIE

you holler as Chad wheels you
down the hall for one more
urgent call.

I won't let you die I holler back
as you disappear,
certain of the next night's mayhem
when you thrash,
jammed in the revolving door
of your crashing ventricles.

LETTING GRAVITY SPEAK

As the nurse raised and
held you upright by your bed
the night before you died
I glimpsed those globes
suspended in the skin of our intimacy
one last time.

My heart thanked you for indulging
the most private ache of our leave-taking.

I recall the weight of
your tilted head and open lips when
all the breathing stopped,
how I kissed your white hair,
cool brow, and tongue's rigor
letting gravity speak.

your body, that splendid machine

SOME CRUMBS

It happened so swiftly
that microbes flourished when some
crumbs of sweet potato mash,
or was it oatmeal with
brown sugar,
missed their turn at the junction
of gullet and windpipe,
rode moist bronchioles and lodged,
defiant of all heaving
in the warm reservoir of your alveoli.

*Aspiration pneumonia
and severe sepsis*

said our son, the young ER doc

*less than a fifty percent
chance of survival*

How you thrashed behind that
plastic mask—
your fraught hands' yanking and tugging
foiled in their apocalyptic protest
by some cursed mittens
secured with bands and ties.

How you wailed,
unable to separate your new anguish
from the old—spun
in that revolving drum of dementia.

Stunned, I witnessed my
white-haired love
marooned in plastic stuff connecting oxygen with
tunnels to a haze of exodus.

Freude, we sang *Ode to Joy,*

O the Mozart and Bach,
the gurgling of *Rendezvous*—our special croon,
children and grandchildren
by your bed
each brushed by your gaze,

your hand,
your grace,

some crumbs still salvageable.

UNIFIED FIELD

—a mathematical theory

with Rabbi Jonathan
we joined hands—you Hillary, Josh
the grandchildren and I,

your clear voice resonant beneath
the ventilator—
eternity's vestibule.

We chanted the *Shema*,
the 'unified field'
of Jews' final witness to God's Oneness.

Are you in pain? Josh asked.
No, you replied.
Our breathing mingled until morning

VITRUVIAN MAN

Remember that lap-blanket ride on the fast
track from our NY nuptials to our DC marriage
bed. Those epicurean Oysters Rockefeller at
the Four Georges. I crave your cradling,

the solace of head on chest, your long arms
and straight legs—artists have drawn you
squared in perfect circles, the signs in your
multiverse raised to many powers arising in

the gyri and sulci of a mind like those alpine
crags you loved. With limbic truth you steeped
the souls of our children in footpaths and
streams, in Staunton battles to capture a King,

in an ode to a frozen lover, in Beethoven's
divine spark, in Vivaldi's seasons, the bliss of
trumpets and strings. As your brain's ventricles
sluiced time from the space of its passages you

fought with cadenced breath until the last thread
of air left your lungs and mingled with mine.
Your body, that splendid machine, completed its
work as sunlight stroked the vellum of your face.

I DIG MY FEET IN THE SAND

at Brackett's Landing
where we chatted about this or that—
late afternoon's glitter still blinds;

the waves churn and re-churn
those same stripped logs with syncopated
suck and slap... suck and slap

From Kingston harbor ferries show, then
vanish under tinted clouds stretched taut as
that pause when exquisite proclaims

itself—and time breaks in the moment
yes!   Now heaven's copper pendulum gleams
and melts into the Sound

the polychrome shimmer of your soul   *there*
suspended—your parting sign, miraculous
covenant the day I buried you.

YOUR DEATH MASK

rendered by God and etched
in my brain, the cool blood of your brow,

head tilted, lips open—
my urge to taste your tongue.

As our children carried you from
the foot of the *bimah*

I scuttled behind and saw your casket vanish
in the hearse for your final outing

through open gates to a pile of sod.
Flooded with sorrow I raised my eyes as

a blackbird crayed *kaddish*
by a pine box carved with a *Magen David*.

When they lowered you swaddled
in your woolen *tallis* for warmth and

dignity, we shoveled your dirge,
thud after thud.

THAT'S MY DADDY

our son Josh yelled standing on his chair
as you strode the *bimah* in your Sabbath
suit chanting zeal into crowned *nigunim,*
words scratched in parchment as old as the
sages who wore them over their hearts.

So when Josh himself, stood in a dark suit
on that same dais forty years later, your
casket on the floor before us, a life span
unscrolled as Aria, his daughter, climbed
on her chair and hollered—*that's my daddy!*

SILENCE

Your voice ringing from its rib-grotto,
soundless now but for videos replayed

like pixel sepiatones. When you went,
our floors were bereft of their reflections,

our walls mute as a dead fly, as quiet as
the empty dresser when the burglars left

and as my ear which went deaf, more than
the backyard at night, our maple glued

black against the sky, as noiseless as our
kitchen in the morning without the clank

and hiss I crave, more silent than stones
that I've piled on your grave.

I SWORE IT WAS YOU

when the sun rose on the green,
silent as the gold gathered.

I saw your shadow by the ferns
and salmonberry near the bluff

like the deer this morning,
a silhouette passing. Later,

on that same green skimmed
by the moon—I heard you howl.

EVEN TODAY

Pungent drift of brew,
oatmeal,
and newsprint on the stoop
with birdsong—
our twinned core
glad at earth's wild spectacle through
the kitchen window—

gravid with new risings of
Salal, Kinnikinnick, Cotoneaster
and prayer bells of Solomon's Seal,
green featherbed.

You enter the boudoir
with the spirit of a cock's wattled
crowing

> *Hi Baby*
> *time to get up*
> *half the day is gone*

SO I'M OFF TO MAUI

again, strollin' that cobbled path along
the beach thinking of how you faltered and
swayed in your white khakis that last time
when fluids in your brain sloshed like waves
through Wailea's lava ventricles, formed by
chaos and uniquely fissured.

Those days we'd sip a peach Bellini or a
spiked ice guava at the cheery bar on our
homage to the shrub of *hinahina*, the *naupaka*
and the *maʻo*—exotica rimming an ocean
with no memory except for the grinding
of rock, thrash of spray,

a wearing, but not away, of seedbed, laid
eggs, a boiling and lingering in chambers with
writhed trunks, wind coiled, stiff-limbed
and at the edge.

DID YOU KNOW THAT WE EMBRACED

after they sunk your casket in the ground with ropes,
the pale pine box wide by the shoulders, tapered at

the ends, and above your face, the *Magen David*.
Earth rained on us, its weight pressing my arms against

your new shape, my nose to the wood's fragrance.
Was it a dream? How long since you'd worn your old

blue raincoat on that last car ride beside me. Did we realize
there'd be no further need of raincoats? I thought of how

we tangled in the green leaves and vines of my kitchen
and spun among the indigo chrysanthemums of my duvet,

rolled on the rock-ridge crest by Kanapali's stream and
in the sunlight of the skin-dipped sea—stung swollen;

how we embraced in river spray on Skykomish boulders
glimpsed by kayakers skirting the bend in the water's

flash—*what were they thinking!* We made love in the
rush of rusty smokestacks racing past the window of

a turned down Amtrak sleeper made up by a savvy porter
for the quarter-hour run between New York and Newark,

and in your office window's beam of dust motes rising from
that shabby tilt-back lounger and what's more—

your navy raincoat on the floor.

WIDOWS' MANTRA

Through a looking glass of gold-banded
hopes, we widows read rings into mirages,
wheel about clay that crumbles

like the tissue of old kings,
hoard relics of conjoined mortality
bearing what we know from room to room

like the corpse of Philip,
dragged from Burgos to Granada
by Juana the Mad.

We plot a path over breakers
blinded by glints of bliss, our nerves,
frayed wreckage.

Chasmai, they call us,
'vacancies' howling at the moon,
black-veiled *lachrymosai,*

salty faces fading to amethyst.
God of a trillion suns, we keep thinking,
send some quirky sign.

BEHOLD, YOU ARE CONSECRATED TO ME

binding in all eyes—vows
hallowed by ring, cup, and seven blessings

becoming thousands until the
last breath of either.

Thorniest is the cleaving and
relentless replay,

seared heart fibers crimped like wicks of
memorial candles.

I mourn the tongue tips
writhing notes on lips when sacrum wings

rise to enfold the crux of *eros*—
what cross to bear

in the spines of its wrecking
so deep the vessels seep poppy splendored

fury from the old ploughed ground of
broken glass.

RELICS AND CRYPTIC THINGS

My crypt is filled with relics—
no gilt statues here or splendid spoils,
no gut-filled jars with invocations

or embalming oils to keep the dead
alive for timeless circuits on porphyry
thrones. No birds or crocodiles on

walls engraved with praise and thanks,
no frozen heads in cryogenic tanks.
Just objects beaten out of words and

forged from bowel and bone—
confessions scorched on onionskin,
some enigmatic silvertones to

scan and digitize, like hieroglyphs
pending their Champollion.
Not much to hoard—a *Challah* cover

wanting beads, a *Jahrzeit* candle to
recall, a Math Society award, an old
green tennis ball

BORN HOLDING HANDS

We argued, hollered, mapped the
facts of our eccentric bond on
yellow scraps of rag that rained

like stellar drift into the cosmic
natter. Our bones jangled to some
multiversal croon. We were a pair

of mattress-quake antipodes synced
by evanescent filament to tunes
entangled in a fluke of genome

strands from different mothers on
a wormhole trip through quantum-
land—born holding hands.

YOU LOVED THE TWO AMADEOS

                  Modigliani of the curving thigh and   tuft
of   pubic hair—
       womanizer extraordinaire.
 Was it that   *aha!*
of pallid breast and belly undulant in   silhouette on
   muddy earth in   minor tones   and oxblood
      that beguiled you?
                             Or soupçon of musk
        seized in armpit *poils*
and ruddy blush high on her   cheek or
      was it her eye?
         I caught you flush when you
approached her   in-your-face   *voila—*
        clandestine trespass on the paint-obsessed
    philanderer

    &
Mozart! of the
        icy sigh   who scored *cantabile*
    for that   appalling Don called   Giovanni schooled
      in come-on   *sprezzatura.*
   Was it that he captured reckless 'Johnny'
                           in a major key—
   so keenly favored by both you   and
      he who 'grooved'
                     on the distraught arpeggios
   of his fine prey Elvira,
Anna and Zerlina
          O   those dazzling   *donne*

    whose *bel canto* thrilled us at the Opera

                yesterday   (it seems)

but in the end that gravestone come alive   as large as   God
                                with icy eyes and   *basso*
                        shroud-like

                                                strode out from
            the   crypt
        and hurled the Don into
                    a fiery pit.   *Sic transit caca mundi.*

                        What a trip!

ONE CORNER MA!

you exclaimed
        before the ink-brushed scroll of
  Ma Yuan.

O the intimate landscape
        picturing that safe, familiar
  corner of a world shrouded in mist—
                          little place of rocks and falls,
        old gnarly comfort of trees, roots
a simple wooden platform gazing
          into the vast nothingness of   bare silk—
a cryptic scrim on which   throngs
       might   rally globes

dreamers play with all of
        history's bones,
                jewels cenotaphs arsenals and   pictographs
                    from   silhouetted hand
to rendering of   John the Good
              from screaming burst of crows
                     in skies with   wheatfields
streamed from starry   space to
        rock to brick to glass   to electronic screen,
   to pyramidal schemes from Saqqara,
Pythagoras   to I.M. Pei   from

       Ponzi or some   other game

 let me
  replay
     terror's   half-silence in a fog   through which

                                  sirens echo,
                    wheels shriek
water eddies around rafts   and gasps
       punctuate the

                        the influx,   howls   swelling for
                the small
dead   flotsam at the edge of froth,
            and silence—

            the shimmer   after   shudder of   guns
    words,
            fists, rolls of   razor wire
seeping and cooling   lifeblood
                                        and fire.

On the white
        pearlescent God-screen
                eons   dissolve
                        among echoes of a dragon—
                            does it bear wings or blow flame?
    its Song,   a dirge with many legs
                surges

                in this silent museum hall   fixed
in a pacific corner of an un-inked world
                            where rain falls on sod around
        a needle ringed by Sound
                                        and crags carry the
                        drift   of

                                One Corner Ma.

SOME LET GO OF BONES

*You once told me that to work on a math problem
you had to keep turning it over and over, chewing
on it like a dog on a bone.*

Sometimes a bone is better buried—
You never buried that bone that fed some
hollow fear gnawing like
a bitch-mother
fixed in the endless jaws of blame.

Some venerate each others' bones—
like those skinless lovers of Valdaro tangled and
spooning away in their skeletal
remains—
eternal stone-age adolescent exposé.

Some love their bones to life—
ancient virtuosi playing xylophone,
teasing tones from knucklebones at bonfire
cappriccios, cave-rave frenzies, and
spiked-club bop-hops.

Pimped-up crania,
cheekless to cheekless on Hallstatt tables await steins
run dry eons ago—others hang around on hooks
like the stylish townfolk of Palermo
killing time to rattle critics at a zombie show.

You never buried that bone in *gan shalom*—
the garden of peace, where feuds fossilize with hatchets.
So now, old man,
shall I gnaw for you in perpetuity
or bury it for both of us?

ENTANGLEMENT

Plague—not a new thing,
ring around a rosie's what the kids sing,
relic of some passé playbook.

There's the two of us, crucial stuff,
you departed, poof, but it's that
'tis of thee'—can't get enough

of this spooky action from afar,
my song caught in your harmonic
strings, don't know where you are.

I hum bare maples in the mist over
the Sound and I'm aware that you
receive me; whistle cloud wisps

at the crest at daybreak, you
receive me; that crow pecking at
a crumb, the eagle sentry of some

shrouded bough, his white head
pivots, I know you receive me.
Narcissi arc to the light at a pond,

there you are, a craft with mirror image
and a trail of wake. I'll be awake
a while, rainbow vapor as fog thins.

I'm quantum spin and cosmic shift.
Entanglement's my game. My
interactions drift in a debris of

background noise, you get the riff.
You spin clockwise, I spin counter-
clockwise. Novel hit gone viral,

these corona blues, playing 'find the
hidden kitty' bop n' waitin' for a signal
from some interstellar whistlestop.

SWINGIN' ON A STAR

Tell me, Ernie—
      from your vantage seated on
that bending cushion by the Big Dog
in the blue,
do I seem small and neither
here nor   there?

      You spooled the rainbow
as earth mama pushed you child-like
for that last swing on this cool playground,
rolled high around the rim of
some event horizon   coasting
gravity's waves —then vanished—
swilled by
a black hole…

      thrilled to say,
      I'm right there behind you,
      baby.

MOON BEANS IN A JAR

Seems they threw us a curve, love, our Alan
didn't leave this sand trap with the fullness of
his years, though he kept swingin' through
a chemo fog and never faltered, all the same

he couldn't rally in the final game. As hazards
multiplied, those moon beans failed to generate
their magic whack, so David and Jerry flew
back and Josh, our son the ER doc, kept poppin'

in to check where that last bean count was at.
Hillary came by to chat and Lynn, best search
guru, slogged through a marathon online
myeloma quest—saw he'd hit it into craters,

couldn't drive it on the green, so he moon-walked
home to rest. Were you staggered when he
surfaced with a broken empty jar or did you see
the fragments in the space-time of your star.

I WANT

you to know I can't cook just one portion.

I make both sides of our bed but yours is piled with
books and whatever appeals nowadays. I'm handling
our assets, you'd be pleased, and please know I can't
throw out those tennis shoes with holes in the toes.

I want our song—*you must remember this* to
syncopate against your ear as it did before your fall,
that midsummer catastrophe carved like *mene mene tekel*
on the cracked hieroglyph of your vertebrae.

I want our three zen stones bearing the moss measure of
a half century's bond to solemnize our marriage bedrock
in their graveled plot—like the single slab of granite
marking the cave of our twinned bones.

I want our children to know you were a child of wonder,
schooled in signs and proofs of initiates, imprinting
miracles in their marrow, and that of their children
and their children's children's children

and wanting, I want to not want

*Some notes in infinite dimension—
phrases appearing and reappearing in
various introductory formulations of
Ernie's many mathematical hypotheses*

the purpose of this note

*
* *

*The ferry un-yokes from the pier again,
backbeat of gears grinding its cabaret
as fiddler fantasies thrum to the ripples'
glitter-play on drowsy lids while travelers
plumb the brine and monitor the flock
of seagulls—frothy chorus on the Sound.
I see the scintillations of your face
mirrored in the window pane, a crush
of memory on indigo I carry with me
when we dock.*

*Gulls grab their bread-bits on the fly,
a timeless act—these birds, they never
die, they sit on pilings smelling salt n'
catch the drift of passers-by.*

to refute some plausible conjectures
by showing that… higher powers…
can also behave quite unpredictably

*
* *

*We hover on a cloud-slurried Sound
through runnels of rain, past bluffs
crusted with boughs and eagles girdled
golden by God's glare cast out of the
sky's fringe.*

*Cars in hulls, metallic red and blue,
cooling on their tires shelter drivers
losing little sleep over that deep sweep
of tectonic plate as they judder out
on the old white and green boat in this
drizzly scene—the whoosh n' jazz,
sync of squawk n' rumble lull the air.
The Big One'll come, but not on this trip,
they're sure, though certain of nothing—
the laws of nature are complete, said
Einstein, in themselves. And God, you
never know what havoc he/she might
wreak, or where.*

and it is both convenient and
natural to answer all the questions
simultaneously

* * *

*Half-a-century of spring's recompense
crossing the quad's oblique paths and
cobbled bricks to muster with minds
hobbled by their old habits of free n'
easy, to hawk a taste for brain grit,
the will to stun with clarity, hone that
dogged love of gnawing on a complex
bone to mine the marrow of a matter,
seize a multiverse of infinite dimension
bent by sign and number—and grasp
the rapture of completing the proof.*

*Two-thirds of a life whiteboarding,
chalkboarding, where the moves are
visionary, hardwon, dazzling, figures
and symbols signal a player's agile
traverse of gyri and sulci amassed
from ancient protein, neuro-whispers,
mogul glee passed on in genome
threads—the body's yen for family.*

to make these theorems, together
with their proofs and some applications,
accessible to the casual reader

*
* *

*Crows—my trusty foot friends rise
in murderous cacaphony, and with
transcendence speckle pavers on the
quad like the pigeons of San Marco,
stroll like jaded undergrads around
the U, and when Yoshino steeps
the air with cherry, rise in unison to
do their field work at the cemetery.*

Prunus pendula and serrulata *aka
'Mt. Fuji' nurture neurons sprouted
by the arboretum's muddy paths
where we played at 'name that tree'
counting petals on a clutch o' gotcha's.
It's all whittled in the vines of our
entwined helix, gist of this rainforest,
love of moss, wild huckleberry, salal,
bogs of skunk cabbage hosting tiger
lily, and that sylvan trio nursed off
logs mapping the seedbed of our sod,
the maidenhair, serrated swordfern
and our kitchen's venerated fiddlehead.*

We consider a class of partially
ordered sets and show that they have
some simple desirable properties….

*
* *

*Rattlesnake Mountain, dubbed for
the wind-whipped clatter of dried
seed pods, Raging River to the west,
good trekking in the forks and lake beds
across Snoqualmie's conduit of parched
stones, summer's stripping on a high
bluff, wind-rippled lake swept flush
o' the season, squall-washed or clear,
glacier's carved handiwork flaunting
deer, weed, scrabble trails, sinking
trails, limestone, granite, switchback,
clamber, one pair o' hiking boots n'
how many thousand feet.*

*How many feet o' foot-cable hauled
to greet that blaze o' snow and sky
when hills freeze n' the fall line's
callin,' runs are easy, grab your parka,
grab your skis, grab your goggles,
one last ride guys before the sun dies,
'cause it's the turn, the unweighting,
the drop, coils carved into icy pack
on this summit, wantin' more o' that
crack siren call o' thrills n' skills,
crystal burnin' on your cheek, skier
face off mountain face—flash o' sleet
before the after-thaw.*

simple desirable properties

*
**

*The after-thaw... cheese fondu, the
chili n' hot toddy rush to rekindle
the gut, crumbcake on a paper plate,
never too late for another cuppa,
always game to take on some pungent
feast of wild n' tame. Dim Sum's our
thing on Sunday's gathering of culinary
meet n' greet, the sweet n' sour treats,
garlicky nose o' riblets simmered
tripes n' chicken feet emerging outta'
steam encircled tins to win a golden
choice award or push-cart prize for
lid liftin' wizards displayin' that array
of palate bait, the wait n' see of what
good fortune brings on trolley-fulls
o' shumai, wonton, humbow, steamed
or baked, shrimp ball, meat ball,
sticky rice—to name a few that
stockpile on the dandy spinning lazy
susan, gotta' have some cannot wait,
grandkids fixin' those smells in their
limbic memories at Heaven's Gate.*

the purpose of this note

***

*I cross the gang-plank's old steel
plates rockin' with the beat, rhythm
o' waves lapping, our familiar crags
and misty banks showing timbers
through slow mo' picture windows—
scenes painted by pioneer women.
We ply these inlets to the wail of
foghorns dopplerized by the memory
of those we heard in '39 when we
gazed at the verdigris torch-bearer's
flame through morning mist and
transmuted the gist of our destiny.*

this completes the proof

***
*****

*The sun's glimmer on the Sound
is met by angels from the deep.
I see you as you see me in those
synchronous flashes of entanglement
tunneling like cosmic worms through
passages from ocean to ocean,
black hole to black hole, miracle
to please, just one more miracle,
and for this, I thank you.*

GRATEFUL ACKNOWLEDGMENT

To the following literary journals where some of the poems in this volume have appeared:

FLOATING WORLD   *Eclectica Magazine*

SUNDOWN   *Poetica Magazine*

WE WALKED   *Aletheia Literary Quarterly*

DID YOU KNOW THAT WE EMBRACED   *Aletheia Literary Quarterly* (Third Place Winner)

SOME CURSED CALLING   *Poetica Magazine, Mizmor L'David Anthology*

ENTANGLEMENT   *The Dewdrop*

SWINGIN' ON A STAR   *Kallisto Gaia Press, Ocotillo Review*

MY APPRECIATION

To those who offered me encouragement and many valuable insights in generously reading early versions of this manuscript—I am deeply grateful: Laure-Anne Bosselaer, Nickole Brown, Jessica Jacobs, Jeffrey Levine, and Eileen Cleary.

I also owe a great debt of gratitude to my dear friends of Seattle's vibrant poetry community, especially *EasySpeak* and *NorthEndForum*. Their constant support and keen listening helped in birthing many of these poems: I thank Jed Myers, Peter Munro, Alex Smith, Peggy Barnett, Mary Crane, Kris Beaver, T. Clear, Ed McMahon, Rosanne Olson, Donna James, Philip Randolph, Chris Jarmick, Ra'anan David, Jeanne Morel, Paul Nelson, Bonnie Wolkenstein, David Thornbrugh, and many others.

These poems are dedicated with love to the offspring who have enriched our journey: Alan (who left us too soon), David, Jerry, Hillary and Josh, as well as Alix, Adam, Jake, Izzy, Maddie, Amelia, Eden, Adrian, Jonas and Aria.

Erika Michael was born in Vienna, Austria, and grew up in New York City where she earned a degree in Fine Art at Pratt Institute and an MA in Art History at Hunter College, CUNY. She moved to Seattle in 1966 receiving her Ph.D. in Art History from The University of Washington. She has taught at Trinity University in San Antonio, Oregon State University, and The University of Puget Sound.

Michael has participated in workshops with Carolyn Forché, Thomas Lux, Linda Gregerson, Laure-Anne Bosselaar, Tim Siebles, Major Jackson, and Jeffrey Levine. Her work has appeared in *Poetica Magazine, Cascade, Drash: Northwest Mosaic, Mizmor l'David Anthology, Bracken Magazine, The Winter Anthology, The Institute for Advanced Study Letter, Belletrist Magazine, The Dewdrop, Aletheia Literary Quarterly* (Third Prize Finalist) and elsewhere. In 2019 she won first prize in the Ekphrastic Poetry Contest at the Palm Beach Poetry Festival.

This volume of epistolary poems was written in response to events as they unfolded during the cognitive decline and death of Michael's husband, mathematician Ernest A. Michael. It paints a kaleidoscopic portrait of their richly textured lives before, during, and after the calamity that led to his final demise.

www.ingramcontent.com/pod-product-compliance
Lightning Source LLC
Chambersburg PA
CBHW031127160426
43192CB00008B/1133